Services of Wholeness and Healing

The Common Worship Orders

Colin Buchanan

Bishop of Woolwich

GROVE BOOKS LIMITED
RIDLEY HALL RD CAMBRIDGE CB3 9HU

Contents

Foreword 3
1. The Theological Issue 4
2. Getting Back to the New Testament 9
3. Rites for Healing 14
4. Communion of the Sick 21
Appendix: Synodical Background to the Contemporary Scene 22

Acknowledgements

I have benefitted from being on the Revision Committee which re-touched the Liturgical Commission's original proposals, and it was a happy experience there to do this work. I have, of course, also gained greatly from the constructive and highly enjoyable cut-and-thrust, humour, rich pastoral experience and spiritual motivation of the Group for Renewal of Worship (GROW) which I have been privileged to chair for thirty years. Another member of the Group, Anna de Lange, who was also on the Revision Committee, has worked through the whole text and given very helpful advice. But the Group has trusted me to do this one on my own, and I take responsibility for it.

St Luke's Day 2000

The Cover Illustration is by Peter Ashton

First Impression December 2000
ISSN 0144-1728
ISBN 1 85174 450 9

Foreword

As I write, the new official services of 'Wholeness and Healing' have just been published in *Common Worship: Pastoral Services*, the collected set of official pastoral services for the years from 2001 onwards.[1] These services replace those in *Ministry to the Sick*, the ASB-type provision dating from 1983, the licence for which lapses at the end of 2000. They are clearly 'pastoral' in intent, an optional provision to be used in parish and other contexts according to need, and highly flexible in length, content and style in order to be pastorally appropriate to different contexts. They follow closely after the publication of the major report from the Bishop of Chelmsford's working party, *A Time to Heal: A Contribution towards the Ministry of Healing* (CHP, 2000), and cross-reference is made to that report below. There is also a complex synodical and politico-theological background which I have sought to exclude from the main chapters, but have set out in an appendix. On the other hand I have given several opening pages to a look at the relevant biblical material, a discussion of which was somewhat lacking in *A Time to Heal*. I have one or two cautions to register.[2]

I have not touched here upon 'deliverance' ministry, which is mentioned on page 94 (76)[3] of the services, in Note 2 under 'Prayers for Protection and Peace.' Whilst some of the prayers printed there are 'apotropaic' (seeking protection), issues of actual demonic influence and deliverance from it, issues which the services do not themselves address apart from this brief note, would require much fuller discussion than can be provided simply as a minor theme in this booklet.

---

1 The full set of services runs from page 8 to page 99 in *Pastoral Services*, and the page numbers from that section are provided for reference purposes in this booklet. There is no offprinted 'separate' of the 'healing' orders, but there is a separate *Ministry to the Sick* booklet, which includes provision for communion of the sick, laying on of hands and anointing, prayers, and (from other parts of *Common Worship*) emergency baptism, ministry at the time of death, and readings, psalms and prayers to be used at the time of dying and death.

2 I suppose I have always had a half-hesitation about the very phrase 'ministry of healing.' If we administer baptism, the candidate *is* baptized; if we give communion, the recipient *does* receive communion; but if we administer 'healing,' it is a matter of enquiry, rather than assertion, as to what the seeker after healing has in fact received, and our use of the term 'ministry of healing' may suggest or even purport to promise too much. It is certainly ambiguous. But I nevertheless do find myself using the term in an unqualified and unguarded way.

3 The page numbers in brackets here and elsewhere refer to the page number of this item in the 'separate' *Ministry to the Sick*.

1
The Theological Issue

a) Creation, the Fall, Suffering and Death

Whatever theoretical future may have been in store for Adam if the fall had not occurred, the Bible faces us with the actual effects of the fall upon the good creation of the human pair.[4] In their original innocence, their bodies are 'very good.' The pair are quite unself-conscious and relate easily to God and to each other—indeed in one sense they were created for each other. Food and space, sunshine and warmth, light and delight—all these also are to hand. Within the limits of the language and experience of those who wrote it, Genesis 1 and 2 describe heaven on earth—man and woman as they were 'meant' to be.

The contrast provided by the following chapters is stark. No matter how the fall occurred, we are confronted with the effects—rebellion against the command of God, embarrassment and shame in his presence, exclusion from his garden, predictions of unrewarding labour—and the first actual sins, beginning with jealousy and murder. The suffering that is built into hard labour is followed by the apparently undeserved death of Abel. Relationships start to come apart, and as they do all kinds of inner suffering march with the physical pains. Death sets in, and all flesh heads towards it, encountering it here slowly and excruciatingly, there swiftly and unpreparedly.

Great Old Testament themes spring from these seminal hints in the beginning of Genesis. God chooses for himself a people in and through the seed of Abraham. They are to have generations of captivity in Egypt, and, when they emerge from Egypt as the chosen people, they will, broadly, know how they are doing in God's way by their physical lot. If they are pleasing God, they will progress; otherwise they will lose battles, lose their way, lose their promised land, and/or lose their lives. God's refining process was to replace the older generation with those born in the desert, and the older died through disease, famine, war and perhaps simply wearing out or loss of hope. Belonging to the tribes they defeated—whether in the wanderings or among the Canaanites in the land—was no fun either. Individuals, families and tribes were swept up into the slaughter, irrespective of their personal morality or actual 'deserts.'

In the fifth commandment we find the promise that godly living will have a physical reward 'that you may live long in the land which the Lord your God gives you,' but that must primarily be understood in corporate terms. For indi-

---

4 As the Scripture portrays it, a writer caught by the fall is wrestling with language (and idiom) to describe a pristine unfallen paradisiacal condition far distant from his own experience. Nothing here depends upon one interpretative understanding—let Genesis 1–3 be a literal camera-shot of a literal pre-lapsarian garden, or let it be code for a much longer development, or let it be an aetiological myth—we may get our earth sciences wrong, but we should still get our theology right by addressing the text as given.

viduals it must still be somewhat flexible in its outworkings—had Uriah the Hittite, for instance, previously been dishonouring his father and mother, when King David saw him off in the prime of his days? Thus it is less than surprising that Job suffers without specially deserving it, and it is somewhat primitive theologically for his comforters to insist that his suffering betrays his guilt. It does, however, have roots in the idea of God as just and judge—giving retributive punishment. Ought we in fact to long for a 'fairer' world in which God would strike down evil people in early days and let the righteous live long?[5]

To be realistic the Bible reports a universal fallen condition, a humanity that is both 'outside the garden' and also has no power to help itself. It is caught by nature in selfishness of life, in damaged relationships, in darkness about God, and in death. The creation we inhabit is itself unfriendly (awaiting its 'redemption,' Rom.8.21), though in part it can be tamed and harnessed—and it can also easily be abused by its short-sighted and handicapped inhabitants and wreak an awful revenge for that abuse, one that may well fall upon a generation not itself directly responsible for the abuse.[6] Even where cause and effect are not so obvious, yet the case is strong that the fall and its corporate implications have entailed a mysterious causal link between the creation and the human race as fallen on the one hand and the apparently random suffering of groups and individuals within it on the other.

We need to tie off one part of the pain situation. Pain begins as prompting—the pangs of hunger tell us to eat, the pain of a cut tells us to bandage it, the pain of a toothache tells us to treat it (or extract it). Without the diagnostic tool, we are in terrible trouble. So to feel physical pain is simply to be sufficiently well wired as to be able to monitor when other threats and difficulties are being encountered, and the more sophisticated the measure of pain, the more accurate the monitoring of health. A natural anaesthesia would be a disaster, as some pain is a proper and even welcome accompaniment of being human. To that extent we may marginally reduce the range of pain which we have to view as hostile. But, with that qualification, the general human state has still been one of random suffering, emotional distress, and terminal conditions—and 'it is appointed unto us once to die,' as from the original rebellion in the Garden of Eden. The wicked flourish while the good are damaged for life in car-crashes, and no divine tariff appears to reverse their state. How then does the fallen state of humanity relate to the particular suffering of groups or individuals? How can this be theologically interpreted to do justice to the Scriptures and to experience?

---

5   We can perhaps half-imagine such a scenario, a stage halfway back to paradise; but on inspection it is not simply an improved variant on the world we have—it is a completely different kind of creation. The inhabitants either have no freedom of action at all, no moral will that we could recognize, or they live in a perpetual uncertainty as to whether they are about to use up their penalty points and be zapped into sainthood or snuffed into oblivion. If this is the alternative delivery from the fall, then we probably want to be spared it.
6   Thus we see in our time the delayed effects of global warming, or erosion of the ozone layer, or, more domestically, the pollution of beaches or the possibility of ill-effects from poorly secured nuclear waste.

Is the key in the phrase 'in Adam'? It describes our natural state—all people united in a single organic body as a single humanity. Let it then be that the fall has introduced a poison into the blood-stream. We then find that sores appear upon the body, arising from the toxic general inner condition of the body, but not according to any particular risk taken by the limb or part where the sores appear. There is a random set of surface phenomena, even though we know they arise from a condition common to the whole body. On a human body there can be a cut finger here, a cataract there, a toothache in the mouth, and a wasp-sting in another place, all random and disconnected from each other—but that is not our model. No, the whole body has a common shared poisoning—the human race is fallen. One limb shows little sign of its condition—another is in desperate condition through sores. The random outcrops of suffering in any one limb are not related in principle to the particular risks that one limb has taken—the desperate condition comes from belonging to the diseased body, even whilst another limb apparently escapes. This is a metaphor, even a speculation; but it fits the revelation of God and matches our experience of the world.

b) Good Health

Whatever explanation we offer of historic suffering, we are not fatalists. The Old Testament majors on good health. Ideally God's people will live long in the land the Lord gives them; they will each be at ease beneath their fig tree and olive tree; God will open his hand and satisfy them with good things; there is health (including calm and sanity) beneath the shadow of the Almighty. Even the hygiene codes in Leviticus are for sensible protection of health; and, if the monitoring, testing, prescribing of remedies, and issuing of certificates of recovery is the task of the priests, they fulfil these health tasks simply because their calling is an holistic care for the people.[7] At the heart of it life itself is very precious.[8] There is a *shalom* which includes household relationships (protected by all the commandments), but it also touches on personal good health, whilst being undergirded by the love of God, the true *shalom*.

c) The Apologetic Question

It is frequently asked whether we can put our trust in the 'God of the Old Testament.' I want to respond by two pieces of logic-cum-exegesis.

---

[7] Was there a distinct medical profession? Well, there are midwives in the Old Testament (Exodus1!), but then they had the one demanding task that was not for male priests! Physicians as such come rarely and somewhat equivocally; the concordance yields three references—one, embalming the dead (Gen 50.2); one, as a useless alternative for a king with an affliction of the feet (perhaps gangrene) who should have trusted in the Lord (!) (2 Chron 16.12); one, where there is a rhetorical appeal to physicians supposed to be (with balm) in Gilead, but no healing for God's people in Jerusalem (Jer 8.22). It is Isaiah who suggests a poultice to Hezekiah—after Hezekiah has asked for a 'sign'! (Is 38.22); and God himself provides medicine (direct?) in Ps 147.3.

[8] Human sacrifice is a horrifying practice of unbelievers, and so is the self-mutilation of the priests of Baal. The prohibition of murder in the Decalogue is but a core feature of the general protection of earthly life by God's own decree.

THE THEOLOGICAL ISSUE

Firstly, once we have taken aboard the suffering of the (relatively) innocent as sheer fact on the earth's surface, then and now, then the great moral question in relation to the Old Testament is little different from the same question today—can a just God really co-exist with such an unjust universe and claim to have his hand on it? And the moral question for today is not, and must not be thought to be, 'Why should I suffer cancer (or bereavement or whatever) so unfairly?'—but 'How can a good God actually be in charge of this so-much-less-than-good human race?' That latter question has to be handled on the largest canvas we can raise—the answer has to be one that embraces the random but widespread cruelties of tyrants of old; that includes the horrors of the slave trade, the terrors of the plague, the slow gruesomeness of mass starvation, the holocaust, the continent-scything assaults of AIDS, the future threats of floods, fire, nuclear catastrophe, and germ and chemical warfare. The goodness of God cannot be defended by the fact that he saved 20% of the *Titanic's* passengers, if the death of the 80% has to be left out of the account; and similarly no survivor of the trenches of Flanders could ever reckon that his own survival demonstrated the love and goodness of God, if the very ravaging of the First World War and the count of its millions of victims are left out of the account. The survivors and their relatives at the time may simply have said 'Thank God.' But the larger question about the nature of God and his providence cannot be resolved that way. A true 'theodice' (a justification of God's ways) is needed, and superficial answers will not do.

Secondly, the issue is made harder for us by the Old Testament statements that God is not just 'allowing' disaster, but is actually directing it, as when he is reported as personally responsible for Pharaoh's hardened heart, for serpents in the Israelite camp, for defeats by the Philistines, and for the sack of Jerusalem and the exile into Babylon. There is a hard apologetic task to be done. But if we believe in a true omnipotence, it may be even harder to believe that God merely 'allows' such trouble by inadvertence or perhaps by looking the other way. And here there lies a great paradox—the theologians acknowledge that God keeps the sinful and socially disastrous in being, yet at the same time deny that 'God is the author of sin.' We have to hold both halves of that paradox at once.

d) Healing in the Old Testament

The Old Testament generally runs with the ordinary laws of nature. Thus in the inauguration of the monarchy, as David succeeds Saul and then secures his own kingdom, despite a strong sense that God is in control, there is very little that could be publicly labelled 'miracle,' save only for unerring good timing of helpful coincidences.[9] The story starts that way—Hannah's pregnancy might be a news item, but in medical records it would simply be that a married woman who had not previously conceived (despite her husband's evident fertility) had

---

9 I except the calling of Samuel by God in the night (1 Sam 3), because this was hardly 'public.'

now done so. Treating the ark of the covenant casually or resorting to a witch have spine-chilling effects; and there are 'coincidence' stories like Saul's donkeys or David's plague. But an editor might well have recorded these events as simply news, adding that God in his providence was founding a monarchy for his own good purposes. Specific unexpected and inexplicable healings hardly appear, and it looks as though the two major Old Testament periods of healing miracles are firstly in the Exodus and secondly in the days of Elijah and Elisha in the Northern Kingdom. Indeed Jesus himself (Luke 4.24–27) cites the raising of the son of the widow of Sarepta (1 Kings 17.17–24) and the healing of Naaman the Syrian (2 Kings 5.1–18), and cites both as evidence that the apparently 'deserving' may not be healed, and the 'undeserving' in a random way may be. In cold terms, we have to say that miracles of people being struck dead, or iron floating, or unexpected healing, all hang together as revealing both the power of God, and his targetted concern and providential action for his people at large, and that this purpose outstrips concern for any particular sick individual.

2
Getting Back to the New Testament

So what does the New Testament say over and beyond this picture? Physical healing appears to loom large in the ministry of Jesus and of his disciples. It is very nearly built into the 'Nazareth Manifesto' (Luke 4.16) which draws upon Isaiah 61.[10] Elsewhere healing is identified as integral to his task on earth—not only in the initial presentation of him in, say, Mark chapter 1, but also in the weight of description placed upon his healing miracles, in his reply to the disciples of John who ask him whether he is 'the one to come' (Luke 7.18–23), and in the Matthean citation of Isaiah 53.4 ('He took up our infirmities and carried our diseases') to refer specifically to his healing ministry (Matt 8.17). The healings run as far as raising the dead, and are distinguished *as* miracles solely because they involve instant visible measurable physical transformation.[11]

There is no record that Jesus ever attempted an instant healing and failed, or did not quite make it. Mark 6.5 says he 'could not' do any 'mighty work'; but it was the context which was inhibiting him, and his own undoubted selectivity led him to healing 'a few' sick people (a result which, being presumably instantaneous, would today be viewed as a very mighty work). For a complete view, we add the blind man whose sight returned in two stages (Mark 8.22–26); but there is no hint that Jesus was other than in total control of the event, or would have been content to finish with a purblind result.

Similarly, the disciples were charged by Jesus to heal the sick and to drive out evil spirits. The record is that they did this with physical results similar to those Jesus provided; and there is only one exception recorded.[12] This instance does perhaps reveal the twelve as fallible, or not wholly predictable, in this kind of ministry—but it has to be set against their healing work generally. This is left

---

10 I say 'nearly,' because the categories of beneficiaries include the poor, the broken-hearted, the captives and prisoners—but not quite the ill and diseased, who, with our hindsight about Jesus' public ministry, might well have been candidates to be named.

11 There are various Greek words used—the most obviously clinical one being words from the *therapeuo* stem. The intriguing and multivalent word in this series is *sozo* (with its cognates), for it can mean 'heal' or 'make whole' or 'save.' Thus, in some contiguous cases in Luke's Gospel, we have in 7.3 a compound of *sozo* meaning 'heal'; in 7.7 and 7.10 two other clinical words (from the *iatr-* stem as in 'psych-iatry' and the *hygie-* stem as in 'hygiene') meaning restoration of physical health; and in 7.21 *therapeuo* in its clinical sense. Then in 7.50 *sozo* presumably means 'made whole'; in 8.12 it presumably means 'saved'; in 8.37 it means 'cured' or 'made whole' or even 'saved'! In 8.47 there is a clinical word again, but in 8.50 there is *sozo*. In 9.1–2 and 9.6 there are two of the clinical words. In the apparently separate case of leprosy a 'cleansing' word (*katharizo*) is used (5.12–13; 17.14 etc—*cf* Matt 10.8)—and this family of words of course has frequent use in connection with both ritual cleansing and forgiveness of sins (as, *eg*, in John 13.10; 15.3).

12 This was the failure of some of the twelve to drive out an evil spirit from a young lad when Jesus was coming down from the Mount of Transfiguration (Matt 17.9–13; Mark 9.14–32). Jesus attributes their failure to lack of prayer, and says to the boy's father that 'All things are possible to whoever believes.'

unitemized in the Gospels (see Mark 6.13; Luke 10.17–20), but it is clearly highly effectual, conducted in the shadow of Jesus' own ministry. It looks as though the miracles of healing (including raising the dead) in the Acts of the Apostles were in the same vein.[13] Certainly the kinds of address—the words of power—addressed by the apostles to the sick were like the unqualified imperatives used by Jesus, such as 'In the name of Jesus Christ of Nazareth, walk' (Acts 3.6) and 'Jesus Christ heals you; get up' (Acts 9.34).

If we reflect on these strands of evidence, we observe the following points about New Testament healings:

a) They are achieved by a direct word (with or without touch or ceremony);
b) They are (with the one exception) effectual;
c) They achieve total physical healing;
d) They are instantaneous, and confound all medical likelihoods.

It is, however, worth adding as qualifications to these phenomena that:

a) There was some selectivity, even in Jesus' public ministry;
b) The healings are a decreasing element as the narrative of Acts progresses;[14]
c) No healing activity is associated with ministering the gospel, converting unbelievers, or building up the church in the Pauline letters[15]—with the exception in the footnote below, his letters leave physical healing unmentioned;
d) Even in the earliest period not all are physically healed. Obviously, death is known (1 Thess 4.13–14ff), and is expected for all earth's inhabitants. Sickness is acknowledged, and is not always miraculously healed (2 Tim 4.20). Persecution and suffering come in random ways (2 Cor 11.23–29), and, although there may be deliverance from it for God's good purposes, it still surrounds believers. But—and this seems to be a test case—Paul himself, seeking healing from some handicap, and fresh from heavenly visions, asks

---

13 There is a classic instance of the multivalence of *sozo* in Acts 4.12: 'There is *soteria* [salvation? healing? wholeness?] in none other, for there is no other name...by which we must *sothenai* [be saved? be healed? be made whole?]'

14 Latterly they come in clusters, with nothing recorded between a plural healing in Acts 19.11–12 (*c* 54 AD) and the unique raising from the dead of Eutychus in Acts 20.9–12 (*c* 57 AD?) on the one hand, and the plural healing episode on the island of Malta in Acts 28.7–10 (*c* 59–60 AD?) on the other.

15 None? Well, there are three mentions of 'gifts [*charismata*] of healings [*iamaton*]' in 1 Cor 12.9, 28 and 30. I have to confess to viewing these as throwing little light, for in each case they are used by Paul simply as illustrative of variety of functions or abilities in the body, rather than as affirming the particular 'healing' role, or describing it, or distinguishing it from other activities. It is true that they are unique in 1 Cor 12 as being the only functions mentioned there which are actually called *charismata*, and this reader is left with a suspicion that 'gifts of healings' was a kind of single term (perhaps like 'health visitors' or even 'healing abilities') which could not be dismembered. It is in any case only one function among many, one mentioned nowhere else, and one the exercise of which gets no exposition or even hint here. The term would, I opine, be wholly compatible with the acknowledgement of doctoring or nursing skills found within certain persons in the church. It might refer to that 'natural' ability known as 'healing hands.' For a larger discussion of 'spiritual gifts' see my *Is the Church of England Biblical?* (DLT, 1998) pp 118–130.

fervently in prayer for healing (three successive times) and receives from God not healing but the opposite—a message that the affliction will remain and he will reveal God's strength in that weakness (2 Cor 12.2–10).[16]

We must add to the picture the passage from James 5.14–16:

Is anyone among you sick? Let the sick person call for the elders of the church, and let them pray over him or her, giving anointing in the name of the Lord. And the prayer of faith will save [*sozo*] the sick, and the Lord will raise [*egeiro*] him or her up. And if the sick person has committed sins, they will be forgiven. So confess your sins to one another, and pray for one another, that you may be healed [*iathete*].

So what do we conclude? First, the passage gives a commission to 'the elders'; it tells them what to do in the sickroom; and it connects healing from sickness with confession of sins. But what do the Greek verbs in square brackets mean? Does *sozo* mean 'save' (which might be eschatological or might refer to a present relationship to God)? Or does it mean 'heal' or 'make whole' (which more obviously mean physical healing from actual physical illness)? Does *egeiro* mean 'raise up from a sick-bed' (as it does with Jesus' earthly healings)? Or does it mean 'raise up from the dead' (as the verb is used of Jesus' physical resurrection)? And how does the forgiveness of sins attach to these alternatives, if confession and prayer will lead to 'being made well' [*iathete*]? It is possible to provide a wholly eschatological answer, where healing, resurrection and forgiveness all come at the last day, and the prayer of faith has been duly answered if the poor sick person pegs out and dies under the ministrations of the elders. That looks like a cop-out—but the question then remains as to whether immediate physical healing promises too much. James 5 is a genuine problem.[17]

Is there a 'Gospel Imperative'?
We now re-examine the charter of Jesus to his disciples—and thus to his church today. The basic command is to minister the gospel and so build his church (Matt 28.16–20). Does this then have a command to heal attached to it? *A Time to Heal* says it does '...healing the sick is a gospel imperative along with preaching and teaching' (pp 50–51). My own reading of the New Testament,

---

16 What was his affliction? My own preference among speculative answers is that his eyesight was damaged, which made his movements hesitant and his bodily appearance 'contemptible.' Thus he writes 'You see what large letters I have written with my own hand' (Gal 6.11), and thus it was that he notes that the Galatians 'would have torn out your own eyes and given them to me' (Gal 4.16).
17 The only reference to it in *A Time to Heal* (on p 249) says it is 'perhaps reflecting the medical practice described in the parable of the Good Samaritan.' This seems somewhat far-fetched and both ducks the problem and dispenses with valuable evidence. The only justification would be that the word for 'anointing' is not the semi-religious word *chrio* (with cognates 'Christ' and *chrisma* in 1 John 2.27) but the more medical-looking word *aleipho*, with its suggestion of embrocation or rubbing.

alongside the realities of Christian history and of present-day suffering, leads me to qualify that quotation strongly, and thus to be hesitant about any 'gospel imperative' to heal the sick.

Just as Christians may be imprisoned, so Christians may starve. Millions are below the breadline in a dozen African countries to this day. Faith in Jesus Christ is often very strong in such areas—but people die. When the black death killed a third of Europe in 1348, believers died alongside the doubting and probably at no different rate from them. Causes lie deep in the environment as well as in individuals—and, to bring it down to local level, it is no good laying hands on a widow with flu, if she lives in a flat with water running down the walls, where it is the walls that need hands (and more) laid on them, rather than the widow. We must not get into category mistakes—the effects of starvation are cured by food, not by prayer-counselling.[18] A bleeding wound needs binding up; so prayer may be a complement, but cannot be a substitute. Health in all its ramifications and its deep springs affecting the whole face of the earth is a prime imperative.

The treatment of physical suffering, with a view to both banishing causes and relieving symptoms, has rightly been part of Christian history. Christians have led the medical and nursing professions, putting sacred value upon human life from the wide conviction that Christians are on earth to love their neighbours. The impressive record is located not only in hands-on nursing, nor only in the skills of the physiotherapist or surgeon, but also further back in the laboratory-based fight against malaria, small-pox, beri-beri, air-pollution and water-pollution. In the scriptural story the Good Samaritan bound up wounds and handed the damaged man over to the care of the inn-keeper (Luke 10.34–35). In the parable of the sheep and the goats, the righteous visited the sick and cared for them (Matt 25.36). And our charter to heal the sick comes to us in this broad way, not simply as a 'spiritual' ministry.

I am making a denial on a narrow front, and an affirmation on a broad one. I do deny that Jesus has so chartered his church that pastors or other Christians today can be confident that they can imitate Jesus (or Peter in the examples from Acts) and say to the bedridden 'Sister, I say to you, arise' and *see it invariably happen*. If it is not invariably to happen, not only do we not fulfil the ministry Jesus had, but we also damage people's lives and dishonour his name. It does not matter whether we can tell amazing healing stories, even stories of raising from the dead, if only a percentage of those so addressed actually benefitted, or only a percentage benefitted with full and complete healing.[19] The supposed

---

18 We could go further on this tack—and it is very obvious when under inspection. If a bad relationship is bringing depression, fear, anger, or paranoia, then, whatever the value of prayer for one person in the relationship, ideally a pastoral engagement with both parties, seeking true reconciliation between them, matches the real need.
19 Nor must we attribute lack of healing to lack of faith on the part of the sick or of their family or friends. The 'name it and claim it' school (or 'prosperity theology') may deliver in California, but can hardly address the needs of Africa.

charter *must* view physical healing as the 'gospel imperative,' so we cannot say that peace of heart was the true healing which came to the sickbed, or that death was the perfect healing of the person dying of cancer. Those are rationalizations, excuses, cop-outs.[20]

But I do want to affirm a healing ministry, a ministry equipped with everything imaginable short of that unqualified command 'I say to you, arise.'

We address the micro-treatment of the individual sick believer, suffering outwardly or inwardly or both. We can now view ourselves as in a battle, a battle in which *we draw on every weapon we can, and throw everything appropriate into the attack*. James 5, whilst it may pose some problems, clearly envisages that attack, an attack led by the presbyters (without reference to 'gifts of healings'). So the full armour of battle includes:

a) All that the medical profession can give;
b) Straight love, from family and fellowship (and this often has to be costly to be therapeutic);
c) Forgiveness of sins (though not, as shown earlier, on the grounds that the illness is a tarriffed retribution for nameable sins);
d) The further means of grace—sheer gospel,[21] prayer, laying on of hands, anointing, and communion.

Paradoxically, we know that death comes to us all, and, despite all fears, that it comes as a friend to believers. And yet, even so, we throw all we can into the battle against ill health—and not just by instinct, but convinced that God has bidden us fight. In the process we may and often do see inexplicable results (inward or outward) where ordinary calculations of the odds might have suggested nothing but decline. So in this affirmation, we do not duck wonderful outcomes—we only warn that such cannot be invariably promised.

It is as we take aboard my (d) above that we can turn to look at the character and use of the new services for wholeness and healing. On this larger canvas we can be enormously encouraging—we have much to throw into the battle, and can genuinely and expectantly look for positive results.

---

20 Am I then teaching 'cessationism'? Yes and no—yes, in that I recognize in the healing ministry of Jesus and the apostles a unique phenomenon, from which no short straight line of exegesis can be drawn to charter us to do likewise; no, in that I simply have the three references to 'gifts of healings' mentioned in 1 Cor 12 and in footnote 12 above, and, whatever those gifts may have been, I no more insist they have ceased than insist that hospitality (Rom 12.8) has ceased.
21 Of course, no-one is advocating glib ways of conning the weak and vulnerable into profession of the Christian faith—but true conversions can happen to those in the most adverse health—and I joyfully add to the list above, both baptism and confirmation as means of God's grace.

3
Rites for Healing

The new rites are set out on pages 8–99 in *Common Worship: Pastoral Services*, though the page-numbering is not identical in the 'separate.' There are six distinct provisions, of which the third, 'Supplementary Texts' (pages 42–47), sets out materials to be used within the flexible frameworks of the other sections.[22] Here I deal mainly with three of the first four sections:

i) A Celebration of Wholeness and Healing (pages 13–25);
ii) Laying on of Hands with Prayer and Anointing at a Celebration of Holy Communion (pages 29–41);
iii) The short coaching notes on 'Prayer for Individuals in Public Worship' (pages 48–49).

The 1983 texts were compiled to draw together existing good practice, to affirm and facilitate the continuance of a great variety of uses, and to create liturgy that was enabling and not controlling. So the process between 1995 and 1999 came at the task of both revising and creating texts on the same principles, in part working creatively from the 1983 texts, but also affirming innovative liturgical ways which had developed in the 1980s and 1990s.

i) A Celebration of Wholeness and Healing (pages 13–25)

This first service provides a broad context, giving scope for individuals to seek a ministry of healing at whatever 'level' suits them individually. It is designed not to be dependent upon the more intimate situation of a regular eucharistic assembly exercising this ministry within an existing—and presumably loving—fellowship. With that proviso, it gives scope for use on many kinds of occasion and not simply the 'diocesan or deanery' ones signalled in its subtitle. Services on these lines come easily within large conferences, special united events (perhaps even ecumenical ones), teaching days on healing, and many others.

Its structure is like that of the communion service, whether or not it concludes with an actual eucharistic celebration. The first main section consists of a ministry of the word, with up to three readings, and a treasury of special readings (if desired) available in the Supplementary Texts on pages 44–45. In a 'once-off' event, one or more of the special readings may be appropriately employed, and the ministry of the word then focuses, explains, and carries forward the particular ministries that are to follow.

The next three sections are entitled 'Prayers of Intercession,' 'Prayers of Penitence' and 'Absolution.' These are structurally situated to give the most helpful

---

[22] For the sake of completeness it should be noted that a section entitled 'Thanksgiving for the Healing Ministry of the Church' is located in the 'Thanksgiving' section of the main *Common Worship* book on pages 50–53. It forms a mini-service on its own, including laying on of hands and anointing.

run-up to the distinctive quasi-sacramental ministries which are to follow. Furthermore, they are not an odd-job collection of items thought important and simply put together for convenience—on the contrary, they are grouped for good theological reasons. Corporate intercession is a vital backdrop to seeking healing, and it begins to give expression to the James 5 'prayer of faith.' The texts for this should be carefully planned and not confined to simply reading the provision from beginning to end. There may well be a case for a much wider pattern of intercession, where the rubric merely allows the particular litany. Scope for people to name those in need of prayer should properly be given, and, whether the backbone of prayer is a series of separate prayers or is comprised of the litany, there is much to be said for using different voices, each one taking a discrete theme. Penitence, linked with healing ministry as in James 5, comes next and so drops a broad hint that forgiveness of sins should be sought as God's way in to seeking healing.[23] The accompanying absolution may be either an existing authorized form, or a new text, of which this is the 'business' part:

By the ministry of reconciliation
entrusted by Christ to his Church,
receive his pardon and peace
to stand before him in his strength alone
this day and evermore. **Amen**.

From these prayers, the service moves on to the laying on of hands and anointing. The section begins with a 'Prayer over the Oil' (which others may call the 'blessing' or 'consecration' of the oil).[24] There are also other comparable prayers in the Supplementary Texts (see pages 100 and 101). The thrust is highly 'receptionist,' focussing on the use of the oil, and on its benefits to the recipients, rather than on any supposed impact of the Spirit upon the oil in itself.

The main expectation of the rite is that then an individual ministry of laying on of hands or of anointing or of both will be provided. In other words, at various points duly appointed people will make themselves available, and people with needs will make their way to them, whilst the congregation at large meditates quietly, prays for people visibly seeking help, or simply supports by silent intercession. Some will be reflecting upon whether to ask for the laying on of hands or anointing for themselves.

The laying on of hands comes first in the text. It is a lighter weight of ministry than anointing, and can be ministered by lay people, though they should have some training and recognition for any formal exercise of the ministry.[25] In

---

23 Jesus on occasion actually treats the two as interchangeable, notably with the paralytic lowered through the roof (Mark 2.1–12)—'Which is easier to say "Your sins are forgiven" or "Get up, take up your mat, and walk"?' But then he was Lord of both forgiveness and physical healing, and could give both equally—and the point here is that he proclaims that he is giving both together as in some way linked to each other.
24 This will not be needed where the oil has been through this procedure at a Maundy Thursday rite.
25 I strongly recommend Carolyn Headley's booklet W 104, *The Laying on of Hands in Parish Healing Ministry*.

the New Testament there is probably in origin no such action as a deliberate and discrete 'laying-on-of-hands'—simply that the instinct to pray for someone was strengthened by laying one hand or both on the other person. We do this today identifying with the one to whom our hearts go out, one whose needs we appreciate and long that God should meet, one whose vulnerability moves our compassion and love.[26] It most naturally accompanies direct prayer for an individual. It has been formalized and made the centrepiece of specific Christian ordinances, notably confirmation and ordination, both of them a laying on of hands with prayer. But its use in a healing ministry lies far back in Christian instincts, and has surfaced well at a time when mutual touch, such as in the greeting of Peace, has become normal and unembarrassed within the life of the church.[27]

There is no question about whether lay people may lay on hands in prayer for healing. For a semi-formal ('out-front') ministry, people should be both trained in principle and for each occasion be specifically invited by the president to assist. But less specific contexts arise, and then people may be invited to lay hands on others sitting near them when prayer for healing is introduced, or they may join in a circle around someone for whom many are praying. 'Ordinary' lay Christians who use extempore prayer may well naturally pray aloud for those who are ill without further official upgrading.

The form of words suggested in the text is, of course, only a suggestion. If the laying on of hands with prayer is being conducted on a semi-private one-to-one basis (perhaps in a side-chapel), then the person in need should have opportunity to discuss that need and identify matters for prayer before the particular ministry is employed. If there is such a discussion, then some agreement about the degree of confidentiality to be observed is a sensible precaution. Hands (or one hand) may be laid upon a head or shoulder, sometimes with an arm surrounding the one for whom prayer is made. At times, with great sensitivity about personal boundaries, it may be appropriate to lay a hand upon the actually afflicted part of another's body. There is no reason why individuals should not receive a laying on of hands frequently; but an addictive dependency needs careful monitoring, and anyone caught in such dependency should be delivered from it rather than indulged in it.

Anointing represents a different category of quasi-sacramental ministry.[28] As an actual physical provision of oil is needed, so there is a mood of more serious preparation, and this applies to both the minister and the one ministered to. Anointing with oil can hardly be casual or informal, but of itself calls

---

[26] Right back in the Old Testament there is a 'touching' (for identification!) when Isaac blesses Jacob (Gen 27.21–29), and a more specific and deliberate laying on of hands by Jacob on Joseph's sons (with a complication) when he in turn blesses them (Gen 48.10–20).

[27] Thus the suggested spoken text to accompany the laying on of hands refers to Christ's 'healing touch' (pp 21 and 31).

[28] I say 'quasi-sacramental' because we lack an explicit dominical command to anoint the sick (though we do have an apostolic example in Mark 6.13, and the passage in James 5 to reinforce it), so we restrict the generic term 'sacrament' to baptism and the communion.

for some planning in advance.[29] The prayers of 'blessing the oil' (pages 20–21 and 46–47) illustrate this.[30] So, whilst there is no definitive distinction drawn in Scripture between the laying on of hands and anointing, that 'weightier' understanding of the use of oil should be borne in mind. My own parish practice was to anoint only after some preparation in advance, so that people had to take note that anointing was available at a forthcoming service (or they might ask to have it included specially in another service), and then receive some counselling in advance. Then anointing implied accepting responsibility for ongoing pastoral care; and it was recorded, with the names of those anointed entered into the service register.[31] Thus the parish staff (and others) were bound to further engagement with people we anointed, monitoring their progress or lack of it, and supporting them in opening their need to God.[32] However, with that kind of pastorally responsible background in memory, the 'diocesan' kind of event anticipated in this service might operate on less exacting guidelines.

ii) Laying on of Hands with Prayer and Anointing at a Celebration of Holy Communion (pages 29–40)

The standard parish communion with a healing ministry comes next and here the eucharistic context is basic. The structure of the ante-communion (not called that) is similar to that of any communion service, and the penitence comes in The Introduction rather than just before the intercessions as in the previous Order. A sensitively built up set of Kyries ('Lord Jesus, you heal the sick…') in effect bracket forgiveness and healing close together, but in a corporate context. They do not relate the penitence as closely to the actual exercise of the healing ministry as in the first Order; but the intercessions remain in close proximity to the special ministry for healing, and the words of the litany on pages 31–32 open up a great range of areas of suffering, and the rubric invites the insertion of people's names into the litany.

---

29 '[Anointing] should be used more sparingly than the laying on of hands, and is especially appropriate for use when a sick person is at a time of crisis' (Note 9 of the 1983 service). This should not suggest that it is unrepeatable—there may be many times of crisis, or near-crisis…

30 Note 5 on page 25 actually loads the advice towards the prayer over the oil happening there and then within the Order, and to that extent advises against the use of oil from a Maundy Thursday rite (an interesting reversal of the trend of the 1980s and 1990s). Thus the prayer over the oil becomes a clear part of the theological build-up and flow of the Order (as with the thanksgiving prayer in the communion).

31 The procedure went further. The set occasions were three times a year; and, apart from other pastoral care, a letter went to each straight after the anointing, asking each to keep the parish staff posted about his or her state of health (however defined). Then, when the next occasion fell due, each one anointed on the previous occasion received a letter asking for a report on how that health had been since the anointing. This in turn led at intervals to a word of testimony at the next service from someone anointed at the previous one. The laying on of hands was treated as a much more ephemeral ministry

32 There is a related question of who can administer anointing. I quote from booklet no 84: 'The Canon refers to the priest anointing [Canon B37], but does it mean "the priest and only the priest"? After all, it also refers to the priest laying on hands! No-one knows the answer to this, and the rite sits on the fence, saying [in Note 7] "other lawful ministers"…It would be consistent with our understanding of communion to allow a layperson to go out with not only bread and wine but also oil to minister to a sick person at home' (p 22). It would be equally consistent for laypersons to anoint with oil from the president's stock in church, just as they distribute bread and wine from the president's stock in church.

Because the structure is eucharistic, the location of this healing ministry in relation to the eucharistic celebration stands out very clearly. There is a widespread practice today of inviting communicants to stay behind at a step or communion-rail, or to go into a side-chapel, for a private one-to-one ministry of laying on of hands with prayer and/or anointing (with or without some spiritual counselling); but that is not the norm set out here in this Order, and it is possible on inspection to see why.[33] As with baptism, confirmation, marriage and ordination, the liturgical norm being followed is one where the ministry of the word begins a service, the ministry of the sacrament provides its climax, and the particular ministry to individuals comes after the one and before the other. It includes its own provision of intercessions, and leads naturally into the greeting of peace—and thus in turn to the receiving of communion as the climax.

There are two vital points to make about this preferred place in the structure, over and above the parallels to the other sacraments and ordinances noted in the last paragraph.

Firstly, in terms of the benefit to the individual, if the affliction has anything to do with internal turmoil or damaged relationships, the invitation to get it right before the peace enables the recipient to come to the peace and the receiving of communion in peace. To ask a sufferer first to receive communion and then go to one side for a more specific personal ministry is almost to advertise that the occasion of giving communion is one of convenience in getting people out of their seats, but is not of itself a place of true healing or reconciliation.

Secondly, in terms of congregational worship, this 'norm' of structure assists the rite to concentrate upon those seeking healing, in just the same way as a baptism or an ordination quite properly spotlights the candidate. In this respect it actually contrasts with the alternative pattern of a series of private ministries conducted under the umbrella of a public service. There may of course be differing needs of wholly different psychological types and there may be wholly different kinds of afflictions or maladies. Great sensitivity and flexibility is needed in responding to these differing situations. But the glaring difference is that, whereas the congregation is being invited to *look away* from those private ministries in, around, or after, the ministry of communion, it is actually being asked to *rally around* the public ministry in this place after the ministry of the word.

I want to expand on this latter point. In a loving congregation, where the love of the congregation is part of the supportive spiritual therapy, then individuals may come in turn to receive the laying on of hands and anointing, each one being very visible and public. This was part of my own parish practice, and was presumed in the request for anointing and the pastoral handling of it to

---

33 To say such a practice is 'not the norm' is by no means to exclude it; and there is reference to this place for it in the footnote to the 'Structure' pattern set out on page 27. It is a genuine option, and it is because it is the practice that comes to mind first in many congregations that I have laboured the point above about a differemt 'norm.' This alternative place is also the subject of section (iii) below, 'The Short Coaching Notes on "Prayer for Individuals in Public Worship."'

RITES FOR HEALING

which I refer in (i) above (on page 17). The counselling in advance helped us to discover what the sufferer was comfortable to have said to the church, and then if ready to do so, he or she asked for prayer accordingly, or, if not, the request was made by a supporter (part of the preparation included an arranging for someone trusted by the sufferer to sit beside him or her during the whole service, and to be ready to speak up if necessary, as well as to lead the prayers). Obviously people might be having terrible inner struggles, the details of which might have been inappropriate to announce. But the key to the ministering in this way was to find that which the sufferer was ready to state or have stated. So the 'candidates' would come up in turn, and a selection of the introduction to the ministering to each might have been of this order:

a) 'I'm going into hospital on Tuesday for an exploratory operation, and I'm scared of what they may find.'
b) 'I have been deeply depressed ever since George lost his job, and I should be grateful for your prayers.'
c) 'You know I have MS, and, although it does not seem to have got worse for the last year, I think I have now encountered new symptoms of deterioration in my legs.'
d) 'I have come here with Eunice, and she has asked me to tell you that life has been a nightmare since her daughter's divorce, and she longs for a true deliverance from that.'
e) 'I have a straightforward fracture of bones in the foot—all my own fault for falling off my bike—but please pray for my full recovery, as I don't want to be a blight on our family holiday.'

I would then have lay people lay on hands and pray extemporarily in line with the request, and complete the ministry by anointing administered by an ordained person with a slightly more formal prayer of blessing (sometimes quite close to the one in the *Common Worship* rite on page 34).[34]

None of the above (which has little claim higher than being an illustration of a careful pastoral use of the structure provided) precludes other categories of both sufferer and ministry to the sufferer. People who wish (after counselling) to be anointed, but to be anonymous, may be anointed at home (or conceivably in a side-chapel after communion). People who wish to ask, on the spur of the moment, for prayer for healing, can be given space for a laying on of hands with prayer, without it necessarily including anointing. This too may include a request to the church publicly, or a confidential talk with some experienced pastor

---

[34] Note 1 on page 40 expects that the president at communion presides over the whole ministry of healing, and, unless there are large numbers to be anointed, it would be normal for that president to administer the anointing. Whilst a mainstream formula at anointing is set out within the service, Canon B37, which provides for anointing, antedated any authorized liturgical text and thus left the question of a formula open, and, where specific needs have been stated, the formula used will also appropriately refer to them.

privately. Parishes have to look at needs—and at ministry resources—and come to pastorally sensitive and helpful patterns for themselves. The structure of the rite gives strong hints, and my own developed practice provides one way of working with that structure. Each point of flexibility and pastoral adaptability requires commensurate sensitivity from those officiating.

iii) The Short Coaching Notes on 'Prayer for Individuals in Public Worship'

The third provision for the sick and suffering is simply a set of coaching notes on pages 48–49. Note 2, which was only drafted after enormous efforts on the Revision Committee to be fully inclusive, is meant to cover virtually all legitimate different categories of people and needs, and sanction different ways of ministering to them. Some of these have already emerged here in section (ii) above, but they have become official. Note 2 has the following groups:

a) There are people who simply ask for prayer, and those ministering to them can only pray in the most general terms. In a 'diocesan' context, this may be the best that can be provided; where (as in a parish) those ministering have a direct pastoral relationship to the person asking, then it may be appropriate to ask in confidence for a fuller disclosure.

b) There are next people who do give an explanation in confidence, and then, if the need is to be articulated in prayer, a confidential context—such as a side-chapel or even a conversation in whispers at a communion-rail—must be found for it. If helpful counselling in advance of the liturgical celebration can be given (as in my illustration in section (ii) above), then it may be possible up to a point to share with the congregation the nature of the need.[35]

c) There are those who will share their need with the whole congregation; and that, I would urge, makes for health-giving liturgical celebration, and strengthens love between the members of the congregation. 'Bearing one another's burdens' is 'fulfilling the law of Christ' (Gal 6.2).

d) The sentence in brackets also draws attention to those who ask for prayers for others, whilst offering themselves to receive the laying on of hands—or even anointing. This has become a regular practice, and, when one reflects, it is obviously a wholly natural step—people are not just concerned about their own health, but also for granny slowly declining at home, or a daughter nursing in a malaria-infested place overseas. In the first instance, anyone whose condition and needs can be named ought to be included in the public intercessions at a Sunday eucharist or other main service, or within a daily round of liturgy. But particular needs, affecting particular friends or relatives, may also lead to this request for a vicarious laying on of hands.

---

[35] See my typical quotations on page 19 above.

4
Communion of the Sick

The next part of the official Orders provides for celebrations of communion for the housebound and shut-in, using Order One (pages 53–61) or Order One (traditional) (pages 63–72). Very little of specific variation from the standard provision for communion appears.[36] The actual celebration and its usefulness will be dependent upon pastoral good sense as much as textual expertise, and situations will vary greatly.

Following these Orders there is separate provision on pages 74–91 for communion of the sick by 'extension.'[37] The crucial theological focus is the 'Words of Introduction' on page 74:

> The Church of God, of which we are members, has taken bread and wine and given thanks over them according to our Lord's command. These holy gifts are now offered to us that, with faith and thanksgiving, we may share in the communion of the body and blood of Christ.[38]

The expectation is that lay distributants will be taking on this ministry. It is a true outworking of their authorization to distribute communion in church, but it is a far more demanding one as they become responsible for a satellite liturgy over which they are presiding.[39]

Notes 4 and 5 on pages 78–79 provide for laying on of hands and anointing to be ministered in the context of taking communion to the sick and housebound. These can come before or after distribution of communion, but it would appear sensible to prefer a place before the peace, after which all present can share the peace and share communion together.[40]

---

36 In Order One Eucharistic Prayer E is printed out, as providing a text which has well-known responses. The wholly unresponsive prayer from the appendix to Rite A in the ASB has ceased. A run-on from the 1983 texts comes in the post-communion prayer on pages 61, 72 and so on—'Send us out' was always deemed inappropriate for shut-ins, and so 'Strengthen us' has replaced it. This variation is also most useful for services held in prisons.

37 The word 'extension' is not used, as indeed it was not in 1983 (which used clumsy periphrases). Whether or not it is used, a careful distinction must be drawn between 'extension' to the sick, and the completely separate (and not uncontroversial) rite for 'Communion by Extension' providing for a congregational service with a distribution of previously consecrated sacramental elements.

38 The rubric says that 'other suitable words' may be said; and Note 1 on page 78 insists on the principle and makes clear the link between the main celebration and this distribution in the actual form of words.

39 This is the theme of Grove booklet W 157 *Home Communion: A Practical Guide*, by Carolyn Headley. I refer readers to that very helpful booklet for guidance rather than trying to put it into short compass here.

40 And can lay people anoint? See Note 33 on page 17 above.

Appendix
Synodical Background to the Contemporary Scene

Common Worship: Pastoral Services begins with services for 'Wholeness and Healing' (parts of which are also available as an offprint). They were originally part of the grand plan of the Liturgical Commission to embrace a large variety of liturgical material under the title 'Initiation Services,' but the General Synod Initiation Services Revision Committee, of which I was a member, decided to detach these services from the baptism and confirmation ones. The Committee then dealt with baptism and confirmation first (they were finally approved in Synod in November 1997, and were authorized from Easter Eve 1998), still labelling those particular services as 'initiation,' but clarifying thereby that there would cease to be in a view a great range of further services labelled as 'initiation.' Thus it was that the 'Wholeness and Healing' were separated, and were then delayed in their passage through Synod whilst the Revision Committee addressed baptism and confirmation. Thus it was too that in due time they were revised and were then presented to Synod by the 'Initiation Services Revision Committee.' But they rank under the Canons of the Church of England not as 'initiation' but technically as 'alternative' services, corresponding (however remotely) to the Visitation of the Sick and the Communion of the Sick in the 1662 Book of Common Prayer. On 29 February 2000 they were approved for use from Advent Sunday 2000 for an open-ended period by an overwhelming vote: Bishops 23–0; Clergy 127–1; Laity 156–2.

That 1662 provision reads to us as from a totally different era—even a different planet. If there are parishes which still cling to 1662 for some parts of public worship (and they are an ever-decreasing number), yet there can be no-one anywhere in the country sighing for the 1662 Visitation of the Sick, and no-one practising the 1662 Communion of the Sick. The Visitation functions on the presupposition that the person visited is under contract to die shortly, and almost says that he or she deserves it. The Communion of the Sick presupposes a whole 1662 Communion service at each bedside, with a special epistle and gospel, and an exhortation to 'spiritual communion' if this provision is not made. There could be no provision for communion 'by extension,' as the 1662 rubrics at the end of the communion service very specifically require that any consecrated remains *'shall not be carried out of the Church'* but shall be consumed *'immediately after the Blessing.'*

Curiously, it was the revision of the 1662 order for the Communion of the Sick which led to the defeat of the 1927 and 1928 proposals. In the preceding half-century advanced anglo-catholics, in defiance of the BCP rubrics, had introduced permanent reservation of the sacramental elements. And although the poker-faced defence of this practice was always that the reservation was done in order to provide quickly and expeditiously for the needs of any who were sick, the actual growth of extra-liturgical devotions before such reserved elements, along with the teaching that reinforced such devotions, led to grave suspicion from the more evangelical and protestant parts of the Church of England.[41] This suspicion, whilst it could not defeat the Book in the Church Assembly, led to wider opposition nationally (not least from Scottish and Northern Ireland MPs), and the Book was twice defeated in the House of Commons. Reservation was the key point of controversy, and, arguably, almost a test case of the directions the Church of England might take in the twentieth century.

When new services were projected in the early 1960s under the provisions of the 'Alternative Services Measure' there was an editing of the 1928 and 'Interim Rite' texts for most services and these were first published in December 1965 as 'Series 1.' Under 'The Communion of the Sick' there was a, faintly amusing, stick-in slip on an otherwise blank page, and it read *'Forms of service are under preparation and will be published shortly.'* It was, in fact, fifteen years before any draft service was seen—after the ASB itself had been authorized and published. The delay was initially due to a total stalemate over reservation on a cross-party working-party appointed to consider this; but from the early 1970s onwards it was simply that the workload of both the Liturgical Commission and General Synod in moving towards the ASB left little room for this item, which was always likely to turn controversial. However, as the 1970s moved on, the time came when the Liturgical Commission itself had no further tasks to fulfil towards the ASB, for everything had moved down the pipeline towards the Synod and publication. So in the years 1978–80 a return was made to the needs of the sick.

In the event, evangelicals had come to terms with 'extended communion' as a fruitful way of uniting shut-ins with the main public eucharistic celebration, and of using lay distributants of communion to conduct responsible mini-liturgies in people's homes.[42] So the communion of the sick went through Synod relatively unchallenged and was authorized in *Ministry to the Sick* from Pentecost 1983.

However, the texts proposed in 1980 by the Commission included two other draft flanking provisions which proved controversial. As the main text included the anointing of the sick, it was not surprising that, alongside it, there appeared 'The Blessing of Oils,' a text which, it might be argued, was not needing full

---

41 To be fair, anglo-catholics had two major influencing factors in relation to the genuine distribution of communion to the sick; one was that their parochial practice encouraged very frequent communion for those who were shut-in, so that such ministry could involve a good slice of ministerial mid-week life, and a series of separate eucharistic celebrations (such as evangelicals urged in line with the BCP provision) really seemed otiose to such clergy—and the clergy only wished to receive communion themselves when fasting. The other was that they conceived it improper (even wicked?) to hold a full celebration after noon, whilst the sick could be allowed to receive communion at any time, just because they were sick.

42 The first known positive handling by an evangelical of the taking communion from a full celebration to the sick came in the (now rare) booklet no 4 in this Series, *Reservation and Communion of the Sick* (1972), in which the first two essays gave warning about the perils of reservation and the third explored a pastoral distribution to the sick. This was an interesting turning point—five years from Keele and a positive sacramentalism by evangelicals, two years from the provision that laypeople could be authorized to distribute both elements without being Readers, and at exactly the time when evangelical clergy found themselves gladly becoming incumbents of 'parish communion' parishes.

SERVICES FOR WHOLENESS AND HEALING

synodical authorization, as it was not an 'alternative' to any 1662 service.[43] On the other hand, not only was anointing now commended in an official liturgical form, but those who drafted the ASB lectionary had brought in propers for the 'Blessing of the Oils' on Maundy Thursday, and it could be argued that the one feature now lacking was the centrepiece of such blessing. But in the Synod the lovers of such liturgy outbid themselves, and the text became so partisanly 'catholic' that it was easy for evangelicals to raise a blocking third in the House of Laity at Final Approval, and thus exclude any prayer of blessing oils from official authorization.[44]

The other doubtful flanking provision was 'The Reconciliation of a Penitent.' The problem here was the 'indicative' absolution drawn from the 1662 Visitation of the Sick, a provision there for those at the point of death:

'...and by his authority committed unto me
I absolve you from all your sins...'

I (along with Hugh Craig) dissented from this, and opposed it consistently from publication in 1980 to Final Approval in February 1983. I did not (and do not) believe it right or prudent that the Church of England should today underwrite a text including 'I absolve you from all your sins,' to be used with perfectly healthy penitents in a far wider way than the narrow range of uses of it in 1662.[45] The House of Laity of the day got the message, and in February 1983, after the first-ever reference to separate Houses, denied this rite also the two-thirds majority it needed. It has not, of course, made one whit of difference to the use of such texts in the absolving of healthy penitents.

Since that day, the Canon lawyers have oscillated in their view of the standing of absolutions. This is not only a question as to whether a particular charter is uniquely given to ordained presbyters to utter particular grammatical forms of absolution, but is also a question as to whether such absolutions have themselves to be authorized by General Synod in a known and limited number of forms before they can be lawfully used.

---

43 The new Canons of the 1960s had chartered anointing of the sick as a pastoral ministry, and said that the clergy should use oil 'previously consecrated for that purpose,' and yet did not either have or even need to have an official text provided for such consecration.

44 It will be noted that no actual authorization was needed, as no service of this sort existed in the 1662 BCP. The result is that up and down the land Maundy Thursday rites for 'The Blessing of Oils' continue, with each diocese—perhaps each bishop—having a different private text. It is, of course, the kind of material that would nowadays be 'commended' by the House of Bishops, and gain a place in official collections. But in 1982–83 that solution had not yet been pioneered and it only arose in 1984–85 in connection with Lent—Holy Week—Easter when a more pressing kind of synodical emergency was being encountered—the issue of an authorized absolution (see note 40 below).

45 If pushed, I was prepared to say that I thought it an unwise use in 1662 itself (though understandable in its context). Throughout the whole exercise of providing services 'alternative' to those in 1662, it was almost axiomatic that we were seeking better expressions of pastoral theology in liturgical terms than were to be found in 1662, and I saw no reason why suddenly a 1662 text had to become foundational to a (greatly changed) practice. There is no space here to look at length at the Church of England's handling of auricular confession at the Reformation, or the very tight constraints on the use of the 1662 absolution at the Visitation of the Sick. But, once it was clear that it was *not* those in danger of death for whom we were providing, then our rite was not 'alternative' to anything in the BCP and did not need the synodical authorization I was so solemnly assured was needed. Any one-and-one, relatively private, personal ministry can be conducted pastorally without its needing an official 'alternative' liturgical service, solemnly authorized by General Synod, by which to conduct it.